Coming soon from Mark A. Willson

## Troubleshooter's Arsenal 2:
## Friends & Foes

## Troubleshooter's Arsenal 3:
## Strike Teams

# Quick Order Form

**Order Methods—**

*Mail:*     Uncommon Technology, Publishing Group
5400 Carillon Point, Kirkland WA 98033 USA

*Tel:*     800.910.9000 toll-free.
Please have your credit card ready.

*Fax:*     800.910.9505 toll-free. Fax this form.

*Web:*     www.UncommonTechnology.com/Bookorders

*Email:*     Bookorders@UncommonTechnology.com

**Please send me the following items—**

_____

_____

**Shipping:**     **U.S. (Priority Mail): $5 plus $1 per item**
Int'l (Airmail): $5 plus $5 per item (estimated)

*Name:* _____

*Address:* _____

_____

_____

*Telephone:* _____ *Email:* _____

**Payment** (circle one):   Check   Visa   MC   Discover   Amex
WA state residents please include all applicable sales taxes.

*Credit Card No.:* _____ *Expires:* _____

*Name (on card):* _____

*Signature:* _____

**Satisfaction Guarantee:** I understand that I may return any item within thirty days for a full refund of the purchase price.

***Please send me FREE information on (circle):***

Books    Speaking/Seminars    Newsletters    Consulting

√ **Be sure to send me my free bookmark.**

# ART PASSION... DENIED!

## By Altin Dervishi

**BASED ON TRUE STORIES**

# Quince & Green

Copyright © 2018 Altin Dervishi

ISBN: 0-9936895-5-8
ISBN-13: 978-0-9936895-5-0

*In memory of my beloved late sister Merita Poda*

*To: All those artists who were refused, denied, and prosecuted, for innocently expressing their talent and passion.*

*To: Canada and all those Canadians who have always open their hearts by helping many of the needy and the unjustly persecuted people around the world.*

*- A.D.*

ACKNOWLEDGMENTS

Many thanks for the great help with the book to Astrit Konica, Bruce Gravel, Sheila Galley, Sue Reed, Merlyn McCarthy, Sarah Tompa, and Fatjona Poda. Also many thanks to my wife Elsa Dervishi and my son Erik.

This book is based on a few true stories. Not everything in this book is the exact true story or event that did happen. Some places, names and events are adjusted to fit the right age group of readers and to make the story more appealing.

# CONTENTS

Dritan, a talented young Albanian artist, was continuously denied the right to study at the Fine Arts University of Albania, by the very strict Albanian Communist officials. This unfair treatment that came at a surprise to him in his early youth during the late 1970's, happened because he was labeled as a bourgeoisie family with "western anti-communist values," or as it was called, "a family with a dark biography" and thus an enemy of the fatherland. As he grew up, Dritan came to learn that his maternal aunt was executed by a firing squad, his maternal uncle was in jail for life, and his father, who had tried to escape the well guarded country, left no trace behind and no one knew if he was dead or alive. Such unfair labeling and chained tragic events, continued to bring all the misfortunes to the rest of Dritan's remaining family for many decades of the Albanian harsh communist dictatorship and kept them in constant fear and humiliation.

Attention everyone! Air Canada to Vancouver is ready for departure at Gate 70A! Dritan who was coming back home to Vancouver, from a work related trip to Los Angeles, quickly stood up in the small queue. After all the required procedures, he followed the lines at the departure gate at the Los Angeles International Airport.

Once on board, a flight attendant greeted him politely and guided him to his assigned seat. Dritan settled down and began observing the people on the plane. Slowly his thoughts drifted to his family, his wife, and his daughter in Canada. He had not seen them in a week. His little girl Alba, who had just begun the new school year, sounded so excited on the phone. He smiled.

Many things had changed over the years. Twenty years ago, this life was totally unimaginable. He had lived in fear in a country isolated from the world.

# Part I

# Sad Memories From The Past

4

# Chapter I

## *Lonely And Rejected*

Dritan's life had started on the shores of a beautiful lake in a small city of South-Eastern Albania. A picturesque but hidden European landscape lay along the borders with Greece and Macedonia. The surrounding snowy mountains and the green hills were reflected like a colorful kaleidoscope over the clear blue lake. Dritan's house was on the edge of those heights overlooking this magnificent scene. Waking up every morning in front of that scenery kindled an inspiration for art and beauty inside the little boy's soul. Since he was a child, Dritan had enjoyed drawing and sketching that landscape and the many simple things that surrounded him. His grandparents had noticed his passion for art. Together with Dritan's mom, they decided to buy him some colored crayons and art materials as his eighth birthday present. Dritan was thrilled. These pencils were the best gift ever. Art supplies were indeed a luxury during those years of scarcity.

This situation was caused by the isolation that Communist Albania had found itself in, since in the late 1950's. As the seasons changed, young Dritan kept busy with his fascination for colors, and with the greatness that nature had to offer. He enjoyed the warm sunny days as well as the fresh breeze and the chirping of the birds. Those sounds, would all blend with the serenity of the giant maple and poplar trees or the wide weeping willows, at the parks alongside the lakeshore. Carrying with him a little folder and the box of colored pencils that he had received from his family, the boy tried to capture different moments of that relaxing landscape. Dritan was left-handed, but that made no difference in his drawings. In daily life, Dritan was a lonely boy and sometimes he did not understand precisely why other kids stayed away from him and his family. He even got a goose bump on his head once, while playing in his street, from an upper street boy who swore and threw a few rocks at him. Over time, as he was growing up, Dritan adjusted to his circumstances and kept busy with his drawings and his artwork. The young boy recalled a time when he was thrilled that a distant family friend, one of the few kind people who befriended his family, had handed him some old and expired hardened watercolors. They were like a candy treat indeed. At once he tore the soft aluminum dressing apart, hit them gently with a hammer, and then placed the colored powders beside each other in a small piece of glass.

With just a few drops of water, the colors were ready. Using that self-made glass palette, the passionate boy made his first watercolor paintings. These were genuinely good pieces. When they looked at Dritan's work, several of the town's artists who happened to be old associates of his grandfather were surprised by his talent and ambition. One of these artists expressed his willingness to present some of the art pieces of artwork at the City's Fall Exhibition. Once the Exhibition officials received the references, at first, they really liked Dritan's work, which was treated as a nice piece of watercolor completed by a very young talented artist. The drawing was precise, and the coloring was a delightful blend of reflections and shades, with the light and the shady angles. However, after finding out who Dritan was, they categorically refused his participation stating that Dritan Diga was an unwanted person belonging to a family with a "bad family background." The boy's hopes were crushed. Although he was already too young to understand the whole picture, many unanswered questions left him puzzled. Why was he suddenly rejected? What had his father's Diga family and his mom's Tregu family done that he was being treated like this? Dritan was angry, wounded and curious at the same time.

## Chapter II

### *A Hard Life by the Beautiful Lake*

In the days that followed, Dritan found out a lot he did not know about his family's past and why they were all being mistreated. Understanding all that painful and overwhelming family history, was not easy. Sometimes, he would sit on the big rocky boulders on the lakeshore, and observe the orange reflection of the sunset over the lake. The young boy used to look deep into the bright yellow and orange horizon and would imagine he was seeing his father's image on the far distant shores. Many years ago, his father Agron, was assumed to have escaped the Albanian Communist isolation, by fleeing through the bordering hills to the neighboring country. Dritan and his older sister were toddlers then. Years had passed, and they had not heard anything about him. No one knew whether Dritan's dad had made it to the other end alive.

Dritan's mother, Bardha, and all other family members, remained hopeful that Agron was alive and well somewhere in North America. That was his aimed destination. She believed that one day her husband would come back to take them, but she kept her hope secret. Bardha had met Agron in her youth, during the college years. He was a handsome young man who had been raised and educated since at a young age in a local orphanage. During the 1920's his Diga family had perished in their sleep by a massive fire. Agron's two elder sisters and his paternal grandparents, were in a deep sleep and unable to escape the tragedy. According to rumors, the fire had been caused by an act of vendetta by an old tribal feud that Agron's family had with another tribe in the district of Central Albania, all related to a property right. However, in this case, the attacking family did not follow the proper blood-feud customary laws of *Kanuni*, as it was called, as everything had happened in secret. Agron, who then was a newly born baby, had later learned that his father had been killed in the fields, while working on his land. As per regional custom, it was the duty of a male family member or a relative, to avenge the death. Those few remaining Diga relatives had migrated to Italy since the beginning of World War I, and the only adult male at home was Agron's grandfather Besnik.

At his elderly age, he was unable to look after himself and thus could not avenge the killing of his son as per local tradition of those days, which for many Europeans was considered ancient and barbaric. Seeing that they were left with no man in the house and unprotected, it looked like the other tribe wanted Agron's Diga family wiped out and so they could lay full claim to their bordering property. A few months later, a massive fire suddenly engulfed their home in the early hours of the morning. His young mother, had barely tried to escape the fire by crawling to the doorsteps, holding the little Agron tight to her chest. While she did not survive due to the substantial burns and the smoke suffocation, she had at least managed to save her precious child. Baby Agron survival was hailed as a miracle. Since there was no other family around, the only option available for Agron was one of the very few poor orphanage nurseries located in the capital city of Tirana, run by the Albanian Red Cross. Growing up with close to nothing in the orphanage, Agron showed himself to be a kind, well-mannered boy, and an intelligent student. He did well in school and later managed to further his studies at the Institute of Education in Elbasan. This place, was one of the very few prestigious institutions in the whole country. It was at this Institute that he was introduced to Bardha, and it was here where together they came in contact with the Communist ideas.

Soon after, they both became members of the Albanian Communist youth movement, against the advice and the wishes of Bardha's Tregu family. In the months that followed, the war intensified and so did the participation of the energetic, youthful couple. The young students ignored any warnings from friends and family and became very active in this group. During late 1943, Agron joined the ranks of the anti-fascist national liberation struggle, and fought against the Hitler's German army. At the same time, Bardha passionately organized many mothers and daughters, in preparing food and making clothes for the liberation movement. Once the war ended, Agron and Bardha, just like other war survivors, were looking forward with optimism to a better future together. However, a few years after, the newly wed couple began to feel disappointed by the created social structure and the unjust treatment towards many innocent families that they knew in town. These kinds of treatments began even towards Bardha's family. The Albanian Communist Party had started *"lufta e klasave,"* the war of the classes. That meant that every true Communist had to distance themselves from their "polluted" feudalist or bourgeoisie families even if those people were their parents, their brothers, sisters or wives.

17

The time had come that many married couples had to opt for their Communist Party, and their spouse. They only had one chance in making that right or wrong choice, and it had to be done fast. Agron and Bardha's family were one of such couples, and they became an indirect target of these attacks and ideological labeling. The tormenting decisions caught Bardha and Agron off guard. To Agron who was an orphan, Bardha's family was all he had. Kreshnik and Shpresa had become parents to him since he had known them. Distancing himself from Bardha's family was unimaginable. In this case, Bardha had to distance herself from her family since she had a brother in jail, and a sister executed by a firing squad. Then after their denouncement and disownment of their families, they had to do a self-critique to the Communist Party local base. Then they had to be ready for any deserving punishment that the Party had to decide upon them, where they had to prove their faith and loyalty to the Albanian Communist Party. Among their friends, they began secretly condemning these unfair acts and decisions that were carried out by the newly created Albanian Communist government. In one instance, during one of the local Party meetings, Agron spoke out against some of those unjust decisions and hard choices, that were tormenting many families.

The authorities easily noticed this daring move. Very soon after, both of Dritan's parents were harshly criticized and expelled immediately from the ranks of the Albanian Communist Party, disregarding their previous sacrifices and contributions during the war. Having heard from a trusted source that "his comrades," the Communist officials, were planning his immediate arrest, Dritan's father decided to escape to Yugoslavia, through the hills bordering the lake with the neighboring country. He had high hopes that through the United Nations refugee camps that were located in Yugoslavia, Greece and Italy, he would be able to go to Canada. These camps, which were filled mostly with East European civilians that had escaped their Soviet-style Communist Iron Curtain isolation, pre-selected those refugees and qualified them to live and work in any of the countries of Western Europe, U.S.A, Canada or Australia. The process of selections used to take a few years until funding was provided by such countries. Agron believed that once he crossed the border to Yugoslavia, with his little English skills, he would be able to pass the immigrant selections and get accepted to Canada, a country, which he had admired during his youth, for its vast land and peaceful kind people. His choices were either jail and execution, or a chance for freedom.

Time was running out, and winter was harsh. Agron chose freedom. He said his goodbyes to his wife Bardha and his two little toddlers, Anila and Dritan, and then disappeared on a stormy winter night. Since that night, Agron vanished never to have been seen or to have been heard from again.

# Chapter III

## Uncertain Times

From that time forward, life changed entirely for the family. They had done nothing wrong, but they were all looked down upon, and treated unfairly as a "family of traitors." Dritan used to overhear bits and pieces of his mother's conversations with her elder parents. She thought that leaving the city altogether, would have been a better solution to escape the gossip, the backstabbing, and the unfriendly glances down from people around their hometown. But this town was the place where their family had lived for generations. Even those individuals, who understood and sympathized with their family, were afraid to greet and support them and avoided them altogether. However, those were just conversations. Leaving their old bungalow house overlooking the lake, and going to a different city without the permission of the Communist officials, was out of the question.

Such requirement could have made their situation even worse. With time, those early life connections that Dritan's parents had created as part of the Youth Communist Movement, had somehow helped Bardha and her parents a little. These useful links had saved them from not being wholly uprooted from their home and sent to some of the harsh internment camps like other people that they knew. Many innocent families were exiled in that way; they were living in horrendous conditions in pig stalls, and cow barns converted by the regime into homes. In some notorious camps like those of Turan in Tepelene, or Çerma in Divjake, hundreds of people were cramped with rows of bunk beds in long drenched and suffocating dark barracks without any basic hygiene. Rats, mice, mosquitoes, bedbugs and cockroaches were rampant, and people were turning blind and dying daily from overwork, malnutrition, and starvation. Those barracks were daily mortuaries and some small parcels of land surrounding those camps, had become congested and nearly nameless graveyards. Hearing of such horror stories, Bardha, who was a well-educated elementary teacher, was glad to work for long hours in the fields of corn and potatoes, with a few local good-hearted farmers, as part of her punishment. When it was windy and rainy, she had to work in the mud and summers were sweaty hot and unbearable.

However, she never missed a day and was up before sunrise to be at work in time and was home by early evening. Sometimes she used to console herself and her children by saying: "Look around! It could have been worse! At least I have a job! I am working in fresh air and putting food on the table!" This positive attitude became part of Dritan's and Anila's life. Since his dad had left, Dritan, his mother Bardha, and Dritan's older sister, Anila, lived with his maternal grandparents. They were all they had. Many other relatives and friends kept their distance from Dritan's family as they did not want to have been associated with "a dark background family" as they had been labeled. Dritan's grandparents, Shpresa, and Kreshnik Tregu, had seen their share of life. After the government had confiscated shops, money, and lands that they owned, their distress got more profound. Their other daughter, Bardha's elder sister Teuta, who used to be a kind-hearted intelligent woman, had been arrested suddenly one night, in a company of a few other intellectuals. She got falsely accused of being a fascist admirer and a foreign spy, due to a close friendship with an Italian army doctor. Juliano had come to Albania for a few months in the spring of 1941 as a humanitarian volunteer to the local Albanian hospitals during the Mussolini's occupation of Albania.

The close friendship and the later brief correspondence with Juliano, who also had some fascist leaning, well qualified Teuta as a enemy collaborator and as an "Italian informer" on the wounded Communist partisans, who were sometimes secretly treated on the local hospital. But that was never true. Teuta not only disagreed with Juliano about the Mussolini's occupation, but she knew that her mother Shpresa and her younger sister Bardha, were supporting the national movement against the occupation and she fully agreed with their cause although she never got involved in either side. In the hospital, she treated all the patients as Albanian brothers and sisters, and as human beings, without ideological prejudices. Also she had openly denounced the occupation, even though it came closely to costing her the needed job there. These false accusations, might have been spread by some fanatic hospital staff with communist leaning, that due to jalousie, and conservatism, did not like the young, and cheerful Teuta, communicating in fluent Italian with a foreign occupier during those days. Without any trial, under urgent orders to "clean the country from the spies and foreign collaborators," few of those intellectuals who had studied abroad and spoken foreign languages, were executed by a firing squad in the middle of the night.

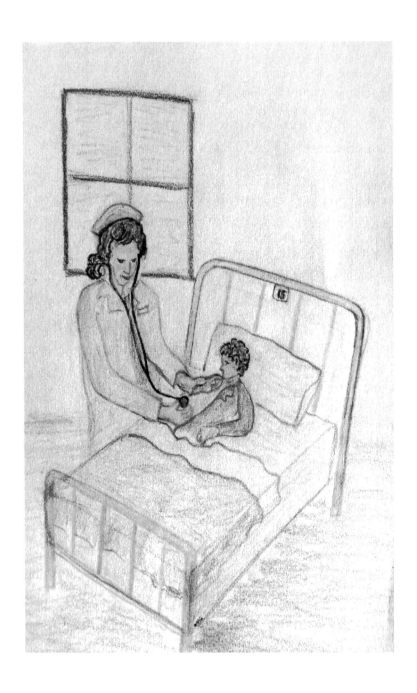

This atrocity, which was organized by the hands of the local Communist commanders, happened so fast that their families and friends were left shocked and speechless. Everywhere there was a fear of trusting even an immediate family member to talk about such tragic events. *Sigurimi*, the State Police, harshly denied any information and refused even to talk to Dritan grandparents, who tried to claim their daughter's body. Over the years, many of those victims' families were never able to find the remains of their loved ones from such midnight secret local firing squad executions. Dritan's mom often used to recall her eldest sister Teuta, with her infectious bright smile, around the corridors of the town's local hospital. She remembered her with her long curly brown hair, as a soft-spoken and hard-working pediatrician, treating the very needy malnourished, and sick children of the post-Second World War in Albania. Teuta had been one of the few well-educated girls of those days, who had graduated in Italy in the early 1930's, and had returned home with youthful energies. Soon after, Dritan's uncle Ilir, a mid sized and well-mannered man, was arrested *"in the name of the people,"* and falsely accused of agitation and propaganda against the Communist Government. These words, which in Albanian translated, *"në emër të popullit,"* were the most used and frightful Communist slogan of those days.

If someone heard it loud while walking in the street behind his or her back, it could make one jump with fear or even faint. Ilir, an enthusiastic and caring young man, had graduated with a Civil Engineering and Urban Planning degree in Brussels, Belgium, in the mid-1930s. He had returned to his home with full intentions to do something good for his people and his country, just like his sister Teuta. What was happening to them was indeed unbelievable. Before, and during the war, Ilir had worked as a road project engineer and had tried hard to make a difference to the severely damaged road infrastructure in those days. With the help of an ex-classmate, a long time friend from France, he had even prepared a tremendous urban draft plan for the future layout of the town by the beautiful lake. Those projects and dreams came to an end and never took place. Like many Western-educated intellectuals, Dritan's uncle did not get involved on either side. He had never been interested in politics whatsoever. Since he was a student in school, Ilir was not a believer in Communist ideas and did not embrace them throughout his life. After the Second World War, the Communist Government of Albania banned all opposition parties and eliminated, or jailed for life, many of these "unsupportive, skeptical, outspoken intellectuals."

Surprisingly in spite of his foreign education, Ilir very soon became one of them too. The "Peoples Court" sentenced Ilir to imprisonment for life. This sentence came as another shocking blow to his family and especially his parents, Kreshnik, and Shpresa. They lost their daughter Teuta, and now they were losing their only son. Dritan found out that his uncle Ilir, just like more than five hundred other innocent and intelligent young men, was working in the deep mine gallows of *Spaç*, in Northern Albania. A very high electric barbed wired fence, from which no one could escape, surrounded the harsh mining labor camp. However, even if anyone was able to get out of there, snipers and dogs were all around. Many of these prisoners were bright minds, which came from well-known wealthy families in Albania. They were mostly writers, accountants, doctors, engineers, and artists, who were fluent in many languages. Their only crime was that they did not accept the communist ideas and sometimes spoke out against those ideas with concern about the future path, which that ideology was leading their country. With the end of the Second World War, and with the triumph of the Red Army across East Europe, the Albanian partisans inspired and supported by the Soviet Union Stalinist ideology, took power and began arresting and executing all the cream of the crop, patriots and western educated intellectuals, considering and treating them as a disease for the country.

Every day these men died of malnutrition, sickness, fatigue, and torture. Extreme tortures like hanging upside-down, freezing them in barrels of cold water all night, to the extreme of drowning them to bucket of feces, were meant to break the prisoner's spirit. They were fed little, while they labored hard for long hours, deep inside those dark humid and hot gallows. They were known as "The black gallows of death."

# Chapter IV

## *Brushes Of Passion Among The Bees*

Years went by fast. Dritan's artwork became more
consistent and more recognizable. That gave him drive and
a stronger determination. He started daily outdoor trips
alone. Some days he would walk along the railway, and
some other days he would climb hills to different
sightseeing spots of the town. The boy, in his early teens,
with pencil or charcoal, would sketch the faces of miners,
farmers, and children he met. At other times, he would
enjoy capturing a bright landscape, using watercolors or
pastels. In one of those out of town events, Dritan decided
to join his grandfather Kreshnik for a bee tending session.
It was a good forty minutes brisk walk to the hills above the
lake, carrying a few things with them. Grandpa kept his
beehives deep in the dense chestnut forests along a valley,
so they could produce good honey. High hills
towering on both sides. Chestnut trees, a few pines, and
giant maples, surrounded the area greatly. Dritan was very
pleased to have arrived.

The young boy missed this place. "Hello!" and the echo brought the hello back to him shortly. He started running freely and playing with his echo for a while, around a small green meadow descending near a creek. Then he felt tired. Dritan lay flat on the grass, and peacefully watched the birds flying high in the sky. The scenery was serene. All you could hear was the quiet flow of the cold refreshing water, gurgling along the rocks by the creek. The young boy stood up and dusted himself off. Then he picked up his small folder containing white paper and decided to draw. Close by, he saw his grandpa who looked funny in his hat and a special protective suit. Kreshnik was gently holding a bee frame and was harvesting the honey slowly. They were flying all around, and did not mind him at all. Dritan focused his attention on placing a few lines on the white paper. Suddenly a swarm of bees began flying low around him. He swung the folder to them a few times, but more and more started coming. While managing to kill a few bees, the swarm got bigger. "Grandpa!" - He yelled and closed his folder up. There was no time to run. Although he tried to seek shelter, the bees began stinging him all over. Kreshnik followed immediately from behind smoking them out, but some of the bees had already done their job.

The session ended up early that day. Dritan felt shivers, heat, and pain at the same time. That summer night, his entire family was caring for him. His quiet grandmother Shpresa or, "*nëna*," as the children called her, prepared a special treatment with some traditional medicinal recipes. His sister would look at him and giggle at his enlarged looking face. The next day Dritan felt better, but his face was red and much swollen. It was sad and funny to see him looking that way. Soon after, the herbal medicine did the trick, and the boy healed in a few days. He was ready to continue again with his drawing hobby.

# Chapter V

## *Grandfather's Wisdom*

Quite often, grandfather Kreshnik used to show interest and wished to see Dritan's sketches and paintings. Sitting on the staircase at the front of his home, he used to smoke his tiny pipe, *çibuk,* and meditate under the shade of the grand old mulberry tree that shaded the yard well. *Rrupi,* a loyal mid-size Jack-Russell dog, quietly stood by his feet. Dritan would sit across from him, arrange his artwork, and explain it at a distance. The wise man always praised his grandson. Sometimes he would ask questions about the artwork and used to give the boy valuable support and advice. "Your drawings are indeed exquisite pieces of art, and you have done them without any help. This skill is a pure talent and passion that you should not lose but pursue Dritan. Have deep faith in your dream, work hard with pleasure and wait for the right moment to seize. Don't get disheartened. Your day will come." Grandpa Kreshnik had left Albania when he was a young man in the mid-1900s, to escape the sudden First World War devastation.

His long journey for a better life, had started when he boarded a boat from the city of Bari in Italy, towards the shores of Buenos Aires in Argentina. After a few weeks of suffering, seasickness and exhaustion, in the rough waters of the Atlantic Ocean, the young man was glad to have arrived in the harbor of Puerto Madera, in Buenos Aires. This place was the land of tango dances and happy people. However, within a few months, Dritan's grandpa had begun to face the harsh reality of life like any other job seeker in a foreign land. During those years of hard work, Kreshnik realized that this experience was not much different from the life in his home country. Every day, the new immigrant would struggle with finding odd jobs for his daily living. Sometimes he would load and unload all sorts of cargo at the docks, cut grass in the fields, or seasonally help in some of the lovely Italian and Spanish restaurants in the downtown area. Months and years went by. One day Kreshnik received a letter from his family. He sadly learned of his father passing. Kreshnik's heart felt heavy and he was living on the other end of the world. "Come home!" said his mother who was left with her younger son. "It could be the same or even better here for you." With the end of the First World War, things had started to become more stable in Europe.

The young man, who was already missing his family, did not wait any longer. In the days that followed, he packed his bags and took the long ocean journey back. Within a few months of arriving in his Albanian hometown, Kreshnik used some of his savings to purchase a few commercial properties close to the downtown area. In one of those buildings, he opened a merchandise store for himself and besides his store came as a tenant, a custom tailor. As the years went by, business picked up and money was not an issue to him anymore. Marriage and family followed soon after. Although Kreshnik knew Shpresa since she was a young girl down the street, theirs was just an arranged marriage and a small summer wedding ceremony in their backyards. The years that followed, brought joy to them with the birth of their three children Teuta, Dritan, and later Bardha. When his three children came to the age of schooling, Kreshnik made sure to invest in their education, something that he had never had a chance to do for himself. He sent two of his three children to "the good schools of Europe" as he used to call the European Universities of those days. Ilir and Teuta did very well in their chosen fields. The parents could not feel more proud. After their graduation, they returned home to contribute towards building the impoverished country.

Dritan's mom Bardha, who was the youngest of the three, studied locally in Albania at that time. She was unable to study abroad like her elder siblings due to the occupation of Europe by the Nazi German Army. Things were going well for the family, and then everything went downhill once the World War II began, and Mussolini's Italian Fascist army occupied Albania. Dritan remembered grandpa saying, "Everyone has a half good and a half bad share of life. It depends on which one comes first." It seemed that for grandfather, the lousy share of life came second, at the end. And that was the most difficult share due to age. The good-hearted man was somehow disappointed with his fate. He always advised his grandson never to give up on his dreams but to find different ways and paths to reach his goals, especially his "passion for art." However, first of all, one had to survive.

# PART II

# FOLLOWING THE ART PASSION

# Chapter VI

## *One Step Onto The Right Path*

Although undeveloped and isolated, Albania had made real progress in the field of education. Considering the ravage that the First and Second World Wars had left the country, the Albanian Communists had somehow done a decent job by offering free education for all. These improvements were noticed especially in women's empowerment and emancipation towards gaining equal rights. But higher education was mostly an entitlement to the Communist elite children and the children of their Communist base supporters. Youth were taught in school "they were lucky to receive free education in comparison to many other non-Communist countries." The teachers would say that: in the "Western Imperialist countries," the kids begged on the streets and could not afford to go to school. With a tight, censored media and only one Communist State television station, these kind of information worked well for mostly everyone including Dritan.

In the years that followed, the young Dritan tried to get into the Art College or the "Lyceum of Art," as they called the art specialized high school. A critical piece of the enrollment criteria for this school was the participation and the achievement of a high grade in one of the drawing contests. The school governing body and a panel of the few art teachers were the organizers of the competition. Even though these requirements were usually hard to attain, Dritan felt very confident and capable of having won the competition. When the result came, he had achieved the needed high grade, but to no surprise, he was refused. This refusal was due to the political selection that was done on the background check of each participant. He was bitter but not unprepared when he did not see his name on the winner's list. Dritan anxiously waited for the next summer contest, and that winter felt very long. When the new summer arrived, he felt more experienced but less assertive than before. After all the intense disappointment, his luck suddenly changed for better, and things turned around unexpectedly in his favor at the end. His patience and determination for the past few years, did finally pay off. The morning of this contest his grandfather Kreshnik, who was waiting for him outside the schoolyard, coincidentally ran into one of the lecturers who recognized him as he was passing by the schoolyard.

The lecturer's deceased father had been a very good old friend of Kreshnik. After a short but warm conversation, the art professor pledged to be fair. And so he genuinely did. Dritan had no chance of being accepted based solely on sound grades and artistic achievements. However, with some quick and unexpected luck and a satisfactory recommendation from the lecturer, he enrolled proudly in the art college. It was the happiest day of his life when his name got announced. Dritan's grandfather would not stop hugging him and smiling. He often said: "It always pays to know someone." The whole family was delighted that Dritan had chosen this path. While in school, Dritan enjoyed the teamwork on many art projects in different cities of Albania. These school years were a very fascinating time for the timid boy. Quietly he began making friends with classmates who understood him better without any political prejudice. Class projects took them to the countryside and many other exciting places. Setting his small easel beside those matured artists and art professors, made him feel special. In the years that followed, he was befriended and guided step by step by their style, and experience. Apart from his school and other extra curriculum activities, Dritan was very busy with his home chores as well. Part of his daily routine was getting up with his grandfather before sunrise.

Together they would walk downhill to the city's market, it did not matter rain or snow, and lined up at the stores to buy their daily ration of one liter of milk per family. Every afternoon he had to do the same for two family rations of bread. Although sometimes he took turns with his eldest sister Anila for the afternoon shopping, most of the time it was Dritan doing these daily chores. All the other groceries were also rationed, but bread and milk were the longest daily queue lines. They used to be extra careful  from the spying ears of the informants called "80 Leksh,"  for the amount of money they used to get for spying around even on food lines. The saying "walls have ears" was very popular. This was the reality for everyone. Years went by, and Dritan finished his art specialized high school, with excellent grades. Soon after his high school completion, he was faced with the same familiar and disappointing reality. His new battle now was winning the tough enrollment contest for the university level of the Fine Arts Academy. Deep inside, he had a feeling that this was a losing battle, but his passion for painting pushed him to continue his chosen path. Dritan completed his (university level) art test, but he continued to get rejected and refused with the REFUZUAR red stamp, for the same reasons as before. While he waited anxiously for a positive outcome, he remembered his grandfather's advice, "Do not give up on your goal, but try to take a different path towards it."

Nearly every day, the aspiring artist would get up early in the morning, and walk to the villages and hills surrounding the city. There he would find some peace and enjoyment, working on colorful landscapes of the so diverse places or sometimes on a portrait of a passerby he would meet. He tried hard to keep his hope, inspiration, and motivation alive, but it was not easy. One windy morning, while he was walking along the lake, he was faced with an unexpected and tragic moment. It was one of those sad events that had happened many other times before in town. Close-by to the lakeshore, he saw several police officers yelling at people to keep their distance from a few drowned bodies. It was a family of four, the parents, and their two young teenage children. They had tried to cross the border through the lake in the middle of the night, in desperate hope for a better life, but they did not make it. Since the lake patrol did not arrest anyone in the water, they had sprayed bullets at the suspicious spots of the lake thus killing the innocent family who was trying to escape the totalitarian isolation. Heavily armed guards strictly patrolled this deep lake, bordering the neighboring countries, twenty-four hours a day, seven days a week. They were using large projector lights to brighten the lake, and could spot anything that would float from a great distance. No one could escape.

Even if anyone ever did manage to survive the random spray of bullets and finally cross the border, other innocent family members were then harshly punished with jail and exile, to remote labor camps. This sad fate was just the beginning for this family circle. Dritan knew that these poor victims' fate was never going to be known. Having been labeled as "deserters of the fatherland," these incidents were kept as local news and those corpses were not given a proper burial. Rumors were that the corpses were sent to medical school for student's surgery practice and their bodies could never be found. Looking at that horrible picture was very shocking for Dritan. It would have been an unimaginable pain for their grandparents and the families of such victims. Just like his grandparents pain for their lost daughter Teuta – he concluded. Feeling uneasy, he moved away from the terrified onlookers and felt sad for many days. Dritan could not forget that image. In the days that followed, the disturbed young man lost his appetite, his enthusiasm, and his inspiration for art and drawing. "That could have easily been the fate of my father as well," he thought. Dritan did not share this event with his mother, who after his father's disappearance, had never fallen in love or gotten married again.

# Chapter VII

## A Guest From The West

As the months passed by, Dritan kept working on his art. Selling some of his artwork below market price, brought him much needed cash so that he could continue buying art supplies, frames, and canvases to work. Art materials were all imports and weren't cheap. One day, one of his art pieces got him in "hot water." This piece, which he innocently sold to a Communist official for a fair price, was titled "A guest at sunset." It showed the black shadow of a man walking, while the gorgeous orange sun, was setting behind his silhouette over the hills. The oil painting was his favorite as the man's image was of his father Agron, coming home to his family. However, he had made a few different testing copies of that dreamy image and was ready to sell some of them. Since he was a child, Dritan had imagined and visualized his father many times in the sunrise and sunset, deep into the horizon, with burning hope that his father would return one day.

But he never did. Dritan had to discover in the hard way why this well-sold painting soon landed him in detention. The official found it to be "very modern," "Western," and "troubling," the terms commonly used by the Albanian Communist officials. That evening, while he was walking near the bazaar, he got stopped by two police officers who very swiftly twisted his arm and started slapping, kicking and yelling at him, without the slightest concern to any onlookers. Immediately Dritan was thrown into an old Soviet car and was taken to a police station. Soon after he got apprehended, the interrogation began. *Sigurimi* or the Security Police, wanted to hear what the "Guest at the Sunset" meant to Dritan. As per their interpretation, they assumed that it meant a "guest from the west" or an overseas dissident guest, who was daring to cross the border back and forth. In their terminology, the sun set in the west, which referred to the Western European and American imperialists, who were the Albanian's enemies during the cold war mentality and isolation. Their questions consisted of who was this so-called "Western Guest?" Did Dritan or his family have any western connection? Were they meeting with, or were they expecting anyone coming from abroad through the tight sealed Albanian borders?

The frightened young man explained through his tears that his picture was nothing more than a reflection of his wish to see his lost father return home. Dritan did not know if he was alive, as they had not heard anything from Agron since he left close to twenty years ago. After a few hours of torture, Dritan was left all night lying handcuffed on the cement floor of a windowless, dark cell. He was not even able to move or attend the most basic needs, and his body was shivery and numbed from the fear, the beatings, and the cold cement floor. That same day, they searched his home and looked for suspicious items. The house was turned upside down and Kreshnik, Shpresa, Bardha, and Anila were all questioned. When they did not find anything of interest, the police confiscated all of his "troubling" artwork. His family was shattered. Dritan had always been a quiet and easygoing boy. They could not believe what had just happened. All those pieces of artwork were simple and innocent. And of course, this left some more room for their neighbors to gossip and blame his family. However, the next morning became the luckiest day of Dritan's life. *Sigurimi*, the State Police in charge, after a rough and long interrogation, accepted his innocent explanation.

Partly due to Dritan's deep apologies, his sincere begging, and his young age, Dritan was let go with a strong warning. It was a very chilling and frightening moment for the young man, whose artwork had all been destroyed. Dritan was thrilled to see the nice sunlight and to be back home in the arms of his loving family again.

# Chapter VIII

## Call To Conscription

After that shocking experience, he began to take things easy, one careful step at a time. Three academic years of university refusals passed. He felt drained and devastated until he suddenly realized that maybe it was high time to forget about art school and move on. By now the young artist had become immune to and accustomed to rejection. He decided to pick up a trade to make a living and keep his art as a sidekick till hopefully one day, the right conditions would enable him to continue with his art education. While he was contemplating his next move, a letter arrived. It was a conscription call from the army. The Albanian Communist conscription, was a two-year mandatory duty for every drafted youth who did not attend the university. Dritan fitted these criteria and so far had been able to push it for three years, due to his university application negative responses.

Within a few weeks of receiving this letter, Dritan, who did not wish any more trouble with the government, had his head shaved, got his uniform, and soon reported for duty. Army hardship and its challenges happened to be a dissent disciplinary lesson for his life. His job was to tantamount to guard strategic military locations, filled with concrete bunkers along the hills and the mountains. In Dritan's military garrison, these bunkers were built like mushrooms on the high hills, overseeing the seacoast where they were constantly watching for the potential enemies. To Dritan these enemies were imaginary. Standing still during his eight-hour service, with the old rifle strapped around his shoulder was boring. However, all this for Dritan it was an eye-opening experience. It enabled him to learn life experiences and to meditate and reflect. The heart-warming scenery of his surroundings inspired Dritan. These were colorful landscapes of the Adriatic, and Ionian turquoise sea, bursting and foaming with fury on the rocky shores at different kind of weather, sunrise or sunset. He loved the salty cool breeze of the sea, which was much different from the fresh air of his lake at home. The artist used to imagine and visualize his brushes, mixing the paint on the palette, some blue and white and some green, some linseed oil and then touching the white canvas with the brush and creating amazing colorful effects.

Some of his buddies in the army, would joke at Dritan's daydreaming moments and sometimes they would make fun of him being mesmerized by nature. Regardless, this did not faze the passionate artist. One day while still in the army, Dritan got the sad news that his grandfather Kreshnik had passed away. It was unexpected and hard news for Dritan, and it caught him off guard. His grandfather was like a father figure to him. The old man had been suffering for a while due to his age and heart problems. In the past few years, he had not been able to travel for a few hours with Bardha to visit his son Ilir in jail. Due to old age, some leniency of the coming times and good behavior, Ilir had begun working under strict supervision, as a bricklayer in different locations around Burrel, in North of Albania. The senior years had been very hard for Kreshnik. The horrible execution of his eldest daughter Teuta, the unjust incarceration of his son Ilir, and later the unfair treatment of his artist grandson by the police, had added to his pain. Only Dritan's family attended his funeral. None of grandfather's relatives had the courage to come and to pay their respects to him. They were afraid of the regime and also they had to uphold their good reputations and to keep away from the "polluted families" like Kreshnik's.

A few weeks after his grandfather's funeral, the boy's quiet grandmother Shpresa, also passed away due to a broken heart. She had married Kreshnik in an arranged marriage at a young age, after he had returned from Argentina, and together they had faced all the ups and downs of marriage. Although their families were from the same neighborhood, they never said hello to each other till their engagement day. All her life, the humble and hardworking woman had been noble and reticent, in the face of family difficulties. Shpresa had seen her kids grow and become successful, and then the Albanian Communist regime ruined their life. She had experienced moments of pride and joy, with Teuta's and Ilir's successful overseas educations and careers, during difficult times, and later it had all turned slowly into deep sorrow. The only child she was left with, who got married and gave her grandchildren, was his youngest daughter Bardha. Shpresa's two eldest kids Teuta and Ilir, did not have such a chance in life. All of this sadness brought a harsh and somber time for the family. Dritan got a quick permission to go home for the second time. He could not stay much longer as he had to return to the army base to continue his remainder of the service. Bardha and Anila were both dressed in black and grieving.

After what had happened they were by themselves at home. Dritan was upset that he was leaving his mom and his sister alone, however, he had no choice but to obey the army orders. By now, Dritan's mother had retired from her hard work in the fields, and his sister Anila, had got a job as a tailor, in a small specialized tailor shop in town. She was enthusiastic about her improving skills and promised Dritan a costumed tailored shirt when he returned from the army service.

# PART III

# A NEW LIFE CHAPTER

# Chapter IX

## *A Breeze Of Freedom*

Once the army service was completed, Dritan came back home. After a few months of contemplating his next step in life, he decided to look for a job. Soon after, Dritan became an apprentice in a furniture factory. During those long hard days, he would come home tired in the evenings, but gradually he began to rekindle his interest and passion for art. Since he was not walking out in nature as much as before due to his tiring factory job, his paintings were mostly scenes and portraits from photo images. Besides his art projects, and his book readings, the young man, would work on improving his language skills in French, Italian and English, with hopes of leaving the country one day. The whole of Albania was like a notorious prison in Europe. In a small population of only three million people, the country had built close to forty jails, more than five labor camps, and was defended by more than seven hundred thousand bunkers.

Those concrete bunkers looked like giant gray and green mushrooms all along the border. Only a very few selected people were allowed in or out of the country. This kind of isolation had continued for more than forty-five years. By the end of the 1980's changes started to happen. People of Eastern Europe took to the streets demanding freedom. One by one, a few neighboring countries like Romania, Bulgaria, Hungary and Czechoslovakia, became newly democratic states but in Albania, the government was resisting change. Young people were being shot while trying to escape through the electric barb wired borders towards Greece and Yugoslavia and others were found frozen in the snow in the forests, and hilltops of the mountainous border-crossings. Among such young victims, was a high school student who lived in Dritan's street. That was quite sad and hit close to home. However, even with all these harsh realities, more and more youth were becoming fearless and were taking such perilous escaping chances and sometimes even climbing the fences of the few foreign embassies and isolating themselves inside with the hope of finding a way out. One summer morning Dritan run into Gentian, his coworker at the furniture factory. He had heard that people were leaving by boats to Italy.

Both men became very thrilled with the news. "My father's cousins lived there," thought Dritan. Without losing time and without any proper plan, they agreed to try escaping the isolation and leave for Italy. First, they excused themselves from work and very soon after, they were hitchhiking together on the back of an old soviet Skoda truck, that was heading to the coastal city of Durres. While driving there, Dritan carefully looked at the scenery that they were slowly leaving behind. "I'm surely going to miss my lake," he thought. His emotions brought a lump to his throat, and he turned his head not to show any weakness. He felt that this summer was looking different from other years. Something was beginning to change. That little summer breeze coming from the lake along the road, felt like a fresh breath of freedom. Within a few hours, they arrived in Durres, closer to noon, only to see the immense crowds of people being pushed away violently by the police. The boys joined this peaceful growing tide of people, that became more and more determined to get on the boats at the harbor. After many back and forth attempts throughout the day, by early evening, a few of the most daring guys had managed to climb through the ropes onto one of the ships which had just arrived from Cuba, and was unloading brown sacs of sugar.

The sailors and the crew resisted at first, but they gave in after they realized that they have no other choice and began helping people to jump safely on the deck. At a distance, the army and the police started shooting randomly into the air and into the boats, to discourage the crowds. A few were climbing, and some others were falling into the sea and were yelling for help. The situation was quite chaotic. All around people were chanting, "The police are with us! Soldiers are our sons!" By late afternoon, the army and the police stopped the random shooting, moved back from the chaotic scene, and became quiet observers of the unfolding events around the harbor. People were drowning; everywhere aboard and around the ship there was yelling, screaming, crying and shouting. After strenuous efforts, Dritan and his friend managed to climb onto the boat using a thick rope, just like countless others before had done. They were soaking wet from dangling by the cable in the sea, but it was refreshing due to the unbearing August heat wave. Very soon all those bodies were melting hot again from the dry air and the proximity. He looked around, and he could not move. The crowd was huge. Men, women, and children, were packed in like sardines. He saw that among the groups, there were a few who were bleeding. They were mostly wounded from their struggles to get on the boat and from being pushed around the harbor by the police, and the army.

However, all those people on the vessel were helping and comforting each other. Among them, there was a feeling of accomplishment and relieve that at least they had made it on deck alive. Dritan was quietly observing around and was listening to bits and pieces of survival conversations coming from all sides. People were looking for people; their eyes were scanning the crowds. They were calling each other, helping one another get through, were shaking hands and hugging.

# Chapter X

## Bari

By the early evening, "Vlora" that had exceeded its capacity, riddled with the army bullets, slowly groaned away from the Durres harbor and headed in the direction towards the shores of Italy. One of the motors would not start, and the heavy vessel began navigating slowly. The water was splashing around all sides of the boat and slowly the silhouette of the city of Durresi disappeared in the dusk. The city's faded lights began disappearing at a distance. It was August 7th, 1991. A slow and anxious journey towards freedom and to the unknown. Different thoughts came to Dritan's mind while he was squeezing in the middle of the crowd. He felt that this journey sounded similar to his grandfather's boat voyage to Argentina, more than seventy years ago. It seemed like migration had become a vicious cycle for his family and his country.

And now, he was standing among thousands of his countrymen who have had enough and were abandoning everything for a chance at a normal and free life. Dritan suddenly felt terrible that he did not have time to notify his mother and his sister, about his unexpected plan, and to say his goodbyes to them. They would never have let him go. However, now was too late to reverse what had just happened. Would he ever see them again? Was the boat going to be able to make it safe to Italy? Would his family ever find out his fate? All these questions came to his mind while he was tightly sitting crossed-legged in the dark, foggy night. Now there was no going back. His mom had suffered enough unhappy surprises in her life. How did he just abandon them like that? She was not going to forgive him for this. The rusty old boat was overloaded with people. On the deck, people were sharing any food and water they had, with the children and the elders. The summer heat was unbearable. Periodically a baby would cry out. A whiff of stale air like a sour smell of sweat, vomit, and urine, would regularly come and go. At the dark horizon before sunrise, the boat captain, who was unable to be spotted among the thousands of heads above the deck, announced that they were approaching Brindisi, a Southeasterner Italian city at the ankle of the Italian boot-like image on the map.

However, he was quickly ordered by the Brindisi coast radio to turn back. After he explained in broken Italian that he had no such choice due to the amount of people, the boat conditions, and one of the defective motors, they convinced him to try docking instead at the city of Bari, a few hours sale north of Brindisi. Bari would have better facilities to accommodate that massive number of arrivals. The enthusiasm among the crowd faded soon. The boat turned the direction north toward Bari with close to ten thousand sweaty and thirsty people on board. Would Bari accept them? Very soon, one Italian military ship and two Italian police boats, began circling at a close distance as trying to stop the advances of the "Vlora" boat and were signaling the captain to turn back. But this time "Vlora" was not budging to their orders. He had explained many times to the Italian port authorities that people were dying of thirst on the boat. The conditions were horrible. On board he had thirsty children of all ages, pregnant mothers and elders, and a few bleeding wounded people, who were fainting at the deck. He could not turn back as time was running out. Although the military ship was trying to block its advances, "Vlora" navigated slowly but determined one step at a time. It looked like it was dancing with the other boats.

Suddenly, a helicopter appeared and started roaming and chopping the air overhead the crowd with a furious wind thus bringing some heat relief. Those loud sounds overcame the babies' cries, the excited yells, and whistling's. The Italian guards could see the enormous sea of hand waves by the people in the boat. They looked shocked and troubled by the massive amount of people. The ship continued to advance carefully towards the Bari shores, refusing the signals and the radio orders to turn back. A new summer morning had arrived, and more boats became visible. As the seagulls were flowing over us, a small line of men and women began appearing at the distant dock. The crowd inside the vessel grew happy, energized, and impatient. They were starting to feel the freedom. A few individuals did not wait any longer but jumped into the sea and started swimming toward the shore. People began sobbing, chanting in Italian, whistling and waving their shirts in the air with enthusiasm. Viva Italia! Gracie Italia! By noon the boat anchored on the shores of Bari a port city in the Southeast region of Puglia, on the Western coast of the Adriatic Sea. It looked like people from the past had arrived and invaded the modern world. They had made it. The isolation and the Albanian iron curtain had been broken.

Such a migration had happened many centuries ago, especially during the 15<sup>th</sup> century, when after the death of the legendary commander George Castriot Scanderbeg, the Ottoman Empire was able to conquer all the Balkans including small Albania. Many western-coastline Albanians, had left their country and settled in the Calabria region of the southern tip of Italy. Even after hundreds of years, they still spoke the old Albanian language and maintained their ancient traditions. However, after more than five hundred years, the Italian people, and especially the residents of Bari, did not remember to be faced with such an unexpected situation. Thousands of Albanian refugees had suddenly arrived uninvited at their door. The "giant" Albanian jail had been opened. A cordon of the *Carabineers*, the Italian police, quickly started to organize the crowds into groups. Some ambulances began giving first aid to the children and the needy, few of whom were fainting from the heat and thirst. As they were disembarking impatiently in groups toward the harbor, the exhausted people would ask around the Italian police and the soldiers for water with a smile. Many of them would look for a shade around, while others would lie down on the hot concrete floors. They were feeling drained out but at the same time relieved for an accomplished mission while waiting hopelessly for something good to happen.

The arrival of the water tankers brought life to the crowd which began pushing each other to get to the water. Then slowly order prevailed, giving a chance to the children and the elderly. Few local groups and volunteers from Bari, had brought some clothes, food and water, for the exhausted people. While the crowds were descending from the boat, the media and the hospital helicopters, randomly continued to fly curious from above. They were taking footage, and were evaluating the situation. Some journalists were doing quick mini interviews here and there, and randomly taking photos of the exhausted faces. The barefoot children who had lost their shoes while attempted to escape Durresi harbor, now were enduring the sweltering hot asphalt and frequently would dangle their feet in the water. Almost half of the Albanian youths in the boat, spoke Italian. They had learned it on their own, by secretly watching the Italian television shows for many years. Viewing foreign media was strictly forbidden in the Albanian Communist state, but people did manage to watch some foreign TV channels in total secret, as that was the only open window to the world. All these newly arrived immigrants, thanked the Italian people and their Government for being very kind and for finally allowing them to dock in those hard moments that their country of Albania was going through.

They all wished to get accepted as political refugees. Dritan thought of adding a few words to the media as well. He had been practicing Italian at home, but suddenly he was blushing and instantly became camera shy, so he did not dare. This would have easily been a tragedy, considering the amount of the people and the conditions of the boat. However, thanks to the good weather and the captains abilities, they had managed to come to Italy alive.

# Chapter XI

## Meeting Mira

Later that night, after all the Albanian folk circle dancing and celebrations at the Bari harbor, the crowd was slowly divided into smaller groups and loaded onto buses that transported them to a giant soccer field called "Vittoria." All around the area, the army and the humanitarian organizations started providing them with food, water, and blankets. Some of the aid was being thrown from above by helicopters, which added more chaos as people began shoving each other, and only the strongest were being able to grab any needed items. But the next day things began to get organized, and although the crowd was disappointed with the treatment, they showed to be more obedient hoping for a better outcome. The heat wave continued to torture everyone on the open soccer field, but after all, they had no other choice but to accept this chosen fate of coming somewhere uninvited. In the following days, Dritan got involved in helping with the distribution of those items.

Among the group, he met an elderly Italian nurse who was full of enthusiasm and fun. While they were working, she told a compelling personal story to their small helping group; "I have my little connection with Albania,"- she said. "A farming family there in 1943, saved my late brother Augusto and treated him like their own until the war ended. He was drafted and sent to war there by the Mussolini fascist army in 1940's. Now, after more than fifty years, my turn comes to pay your country back,"- she said jokingly. Dritan learned that for close to two years, her brother, the young Italian soldier, had deserted the Mussolini's fascist army. At the end of the war, Augusto had safely returned home to Italy with a fluent Albanian. Very soon after, the borders in Albania were closed for good, and than he, like many others, did not have the chance to return and thank those families again. Augusto had died a few years ago, but his family never forgot those Albanians' kindness. Now nearly after half a century later, the chance had brought his sister to return a favor in a humanitarian cause as a token of appreciation. "The circle of a good deed goes a long way," -Dritan thought. Similarly like Augusto and many other Italians, the Albanian custom of honoring and protecting your guest played a significant role in shielding from harm and hiding, many unfortunate Jewish families during those difficult times of the World War II.

They safeguarded the local Albanian-Jewish population, as well as those who arrived terrified from North of Europe by adopting them to their families and their communities. To camouflage them from harm, the hosts changed their guests names to Albanian names, clothed them with their traditional costumes, and crash coursed them to a quick learning of the Albanian language, so they could be ready for the unexpected controls until the end of the Nazi danger. Most of those families came back after fifty over years, looking to thank their saviors. "Humans have always shown the soft side in difficult days,"- he thought. In the food distribution section, among the Red Cross personnel, there were some volunteers among the refugees. While Dritan was helping around, he noticed a sweet looking young Albanian girl, who spoke fluent Italian and was acting as a professional translator among the crowds. He found a chance to introduce himself and as the days passed by, slowly began to get more curious about her. Mira, a slim, average size vivid brunette, with a head full of curls, was in her early twenties. She came from Durres, the city where their boat journey had begun. The cute translator, who had attracted the attention of many guys at the camp, was a second year student, specializing in the Italian language at the Foreign Language Faculty in Tirana.

Her desire to see Italy and to escape the isolation of Albania, had made her and a few of her classmates, to quit their studies and take the boat to Italy. Mira had not informed her parents about the immediate plan, because she was convinced that they would have never let her go. The youngest in her family with two other elder brothers, she was one of those privileged children who grew up having a phone at home, unlike ordinary Albanians. Her father was a well-known doctor, specialized in endocrinology for the Tirana region, where he would commute daily from Durres. Dr. Agim Noga, was among the handful of medics students, who had graduated in Moscow in the late ninety fifties, when Albania had a good relations with the Soviet Union. Although he was a member of the Albanian Communist Party, he had tried to keep a low profile and was mainly concerned with his duty as a doctor towards his patients. His wife Diana, a Czech national, was a head nurse in a local hospital in Durres. After falling in love with Agim during their student years in Moscow, Diana blinded by emotions, had decided to abandon her medical studies and follow him to Albania. When she arrived there, Diana fell in love again but this time with Albanian Riviera. She learned the language, created her family, and adapted very well in the Durresi region.

Over the years, she slowly lost touch with her country, known then as Czechoslovakia. Her Czech parents were deeply angry and disappointment with her decision to quit one of the most prestigious medical schools in Moscow just because of a romance with an Albanian guy. Due to that reason they did not want to communicate with her any longer until she changed her mind. But another reason not to keep in touch with family, old Czech friends and relatives, was also to avoid the suspicion that the Albanian Communist censorship had towards foreigners. And now her daughter's (Mira) escape to Italy had undoubtedly placed Diana and especially Dr. Agim in a difficult situation in front of his Communist colleagues at the Party Organization. However, after their emotional phone conversation, Mira's parents had sounded more concern for her wellbeing and were pleading for her to return home as soon as she could as she was fully forgiven. This forgiveness and together with her disappointment for what she had found in Italy so far, had made Mira reconsider her return home. After she had hung up the public phone, she felt that now she was missing her family even more. She thought that she had acted in her own, just like her Czech mother when she decided to settle in Albania without her parents approval, during her student years in Russia. "The apple does not fall far from the tree"- Mira thought, and smiled.

In the meantime, she kept busy and was making herself useful with her Italian fluency and with her caring personality by helping with the food distributions to the refugees. Dritan grew very fond of Mira's easy going and hard working nature. Day by day their friendship became stronger. It was the first time that he felt close to someone.

# Chapter XII

## Home Again

Days started to go by, and the exhaustion and the worry about their uncertain fate began to take its toll. The setup camp inside the green soccer field was a mess, and the people were feeling frustrated. This situation sounded like a never-ending scenario. In the meantime, the host country was debating on whether to keep all these unforeseen and unexpected Albanians refugees or to send them back. If they accommodated them well, the Italians feared that more people and more boats would be coming from Albania or from other East European Communist countries. An example had to be set. There were rumors that the Albanian Communist Government had promised not to punish anyone who had escaped, and they were going to make democratic reforms and changes for better. But this news was not encouraging. These refugees had lost faith in the Albanian dictatorial Communist system. Most of them came from families who had suffered a lot during more than forty years of unfair punishment and isolation in jails and labor camps.

Within a few stressful and emotional days, the Italian government decided to help and accommodate only those who had family and friends abroad who were willing to sponsor them. Those families had to agree to provide aid and support for the immigrants until they were fully settled. The rest were going to be repatriated back home again. The crowd of thousands of people was disappointed. Few of them started running amok and trying to make plans to escape the soccer field. Without losing time, Dritan decided to try to get in touch with the cousins of his deceased father. Maybe they could help me stay, he thought, but first, I must find a way to notify my family. He felt that he had suddenly abandoned them for a better life of his own, and that guilty feeling made him miss them even more. He began looking for a public phone, as did many other people. The lines were long. After queuing up behind a phone booth inside the stadium, he was finally connected to the central Albanian operator. First a pause and some crackling phone noise and then a dial tone. The young man was suddenly glad to hear an *"Alo"* from the other side, which felt so different from before. It was the first time he had left his country and felt so far away from home. Quickly the Tirana main operator transferred him to the local post office of Dritan's town. Dritan introduced himself to the local operator who sounded like a pleasant middle-aged woman.

Briefly, he explained his situation and passed the message to his family. Dritan felt good that she happened to know his mother. The friendly voice assured him that she was surely going to inform Bardha. He felt somehow relieved that his mom was going to get the news, although three days after his departure. The next phone call was to his Italian Diga cousins. Dritan had always remembered several of their names from the letters his family had received years ago. With some help from an Italian volunteer, he searched his cousins' last name in a phone directory and found their phone number. These were paternal relatives that had left for Italy after the First World War in the late 1920's, but they still carried the same surname as Dritan. His father had found about them with some guidance from his maternal tribe that he had connected with, after the orphanage. Since then, he had decided to reach them and corresponded with a few letters during the time that he was a young college student before the World War II. Then things changed after the war, and the Albanian police, which had a strict censorship, were not fond of correspondence from abroad. During those days, anyone corresponding outside the country could have easily been labeled as a foreign spy. The envelopes were kept hidden in an old tin box at home. While growing up, Dritan had looked the faded yellow letters in blue ink.

Such correspondence from the Diga relatives from abroad was treated like treasures from the outside world. And now after more than sixty years, he might hear the voice that had written those letters and maybe later will meet with all of them. He felt a thrill go down his spine. But that "pronto," on the other end of the line, was a disappointing one. His Italian third cousin, sounded distant and cold and did not show any interest in Dritan or his family history. He seemed disappointed that nearly the whole Albania had landed in his country. After only a short conversation, his relative excused himself coldly. This talk sounded strange, he thought. Listening to that tone of voice, Dritan did not feel like engaging in the conversation any longer, or for directly asking for any kind of help, even though he had found the right family. Perhaps these Diga cousins who were born and raised in Italy, did not want anything to do with their old roots of blood feud and vendetta that they had escaped from, more than half a century ago. Or maybe they did not want to have anything to do with him, a newly arrived boat refugee. Rightfully they could have been afraid that all these kinds of refugees would open the flood gates to more people and more cousins from the distant shores. Shortly after, the tense conversation ended with a cold "grazie."

# Chapter XIII

## Staying Or Leaving

Dritan felt astounded that he had tried in vain to reconnect with a lost part of his father's family. Indeed, his dad Agron would have been very proud of his good efforts. After he had hung up the phone, the young man felt frustrated. He had never imagined this. What should he do? He thought of his mother and his sister that he had left alone. How impatient and irrational he had been, but he could not even dare to go back now. It was a sure thing that jail would be waiting for him. "Just another Motherland traitor from his family"- the Communist officials were going to say. However, from the bits of pieces of the Albanian refugees there, Dritan had heard that the events in Albania were changing rapidly. Everywhere people had taken to the streets demanding freedom and democracy. University students were negotiating reforms with the government. It seemed as though, for the first time, real changes were on the way. Maybe if things will turn for the better then I will go back, Dritan thought.

However, his factory friend Gentian, did not want to go back. "Go back again after all this sacrifice we made...?" he said. "Are you out of your mind?" That night, Gentian escaped the soccer stadium, like many others, hoping to find work in his furniture-making trade anywhere in Italy or somewhere in Europe. He said his goodbyes to Dritan and left in the early hours of the morning. Many years after, Dritan heard that Gentian had settled in Austria and found work as a furniture apprentice for a few years. With experience, he became a successful furniture maker and later built his house in a beautiful Austrian border town next to Northern Italy. After parting good-bye with his hometown friend, Dritan decided to go back. To him, the whole story of risking his life, taking a boat and coming to Italy without telling his lonely mother and sister, now seemed foolish. However, it happened. It was time to correct his mistakes and move on. After all, he and Mira had become excellent friends and together had agreed to return home. Dritan was secretly in love with her, and he felt that Mira had the same feelings, but something was bothering him. Was his family ready to accept the daughter of a Communist? This relationship could have been unacceptable for Mira's parents since Dritan came from a family with "a dark past" with an uncle in jail as a political prisoner.

What about his uncle that was still in prison? How would he feel of this relationship? Dritan felt blinded by love, but he believed that even though Mira's father was a member of Communist Party in Durresi hospital, as per Mira, her parents did not get involved in politics. They were family oriented and helpful towards the people who needed help especially with the sick patients at the hospital. Years ago they also had been part of such punishment by the system and had paid their dues. During their lengthy discussions at the temporary refugee camp, they had both agreed that for more than forty years, the Albanian Communist Party dictatorship had terrorized the innocent people and isolated Albania from the world. Mira's outgoing personality, as well as the love to see the world, had brought her with a quick decision to abandon her studies and end up in Italy without her parents' permission. Dritan had strong feelings for her and things were looking well so far, so he decided to tread carefully and move one step at a time. He took a deep breath and felt sorry that he would not have the chance to live in and to explore the beauty of Rome, Florence, Milan, Venice. They were on the central and northern part of Italy quite a far drive from the south western city of Bari. The young artist wanted to see the thrilling Coliseum Arena, the Pantheon temple, the Uffizi gallery, Palazzo Vecchio, Sforzza Castle, and few of the different Piazzas around. These places could have offered a new world of art and beauty for Dritan. They were a blend of history, of the past, and of the present as he had read and learned about those masterpieces in school. Rafael, Da Vinci, the Medici's, Michelangelo, Sforzza and so many more. The next afternoon, Dritan heard from the mini gatherings at the stadium that Communism had collapsed in Albania. Crowds in Tirana, had gathered and dragged the statue of the dictator to the ground. A new multi-party democracy was taking the leadership of the impoverished country. People were gathering all around the city squares of the different Albanian towns and were one by one toppling the statues of the Albanian Communist dictator as well as other symbols of that long and hard dictatorial system. The Italian Government had decided fly home all the rest of the refugees that were not able to find a sponsor. Dritan called his hometown post office again and left news for his mother that he was coming home. It was his first time on a plane, and the flight besides Mira was fast and comfortable. At the small old Tirana airport, he was braced for one surprise after another. First, he was forgiven and greeted and hugged by his mother, his newly engaged sister together with her fiancé Alban, and lastly, his uncle Ilir, who had spent all his life in jail.

Dritan became emotional and could not hold back his tears. This unfortunate man was standing tall and fragile with his snow-white hair right in front of him. He could see very deep wrinkles in his thin face. It was the face of endurance. Those eyes that had seen a lot of suffering, were beaming with a happy glow. The innocent and good-hearted man had suffered unjustly for decades and had survived all those horrible years. It was unbelievable; He had nothing else left except his sister Bardha (Dritan's mom), and her family. They hugged and cried into each other's arms, and did not stop talking all along the way home. Mira also met with them at the airport, and soon she excused herself to look for her family. It seemed that Dritan's mom and his sister, liked Mira, as they gave her a big hug and later would not stop teasing him about her. However, Dritan was being careful and had decided to talk about Mira another day. Now that Albanian Communism had collapsed, and changes were taking place, he did not think that Mira's father would object about Dritan's family background any longer. Those days of digging into people's family lives were gone. The only issue at the time was how his mom Bardha and his uncle Ilir would react on finding out that Mira was the daughter of a Communist Party member.

However, even Dritan's father had been a Party member before his disappearance. Now that times were changing, people had become forgiving towards the past and were looking more hopeful towards the free and equal future. Dritan recalled some time ago, when as a small boy with his mother and grandparents, he used to visit his uncle in jail. He would never forget those supervised short emotionally charged meetings, where his mother would brink uncle Ilir wool socks, mittens and scarfs, that she and grandma Shpresa had knit together to protect him from the hard wok in the harsh cold northern weather. With time, his uncle had moved out of the notorious mines and for good behavior was working as a bricklayer, building apartments around the northern region. However, he was always bitter with the unjust lifetime punishment he had received just for studying abroad. In one of those visits, Dritan overheard his uncle whispering quietly to his mother Bardha. "Hang on there sister. Don't worry about me. We are all closed up in a giant jail. Mine is just a mini jail inside the big one. I will be ok." Those words got stuck in Dritan 's head, just like a morning song that you can't forget for days. A small box inside the giant box…Finally, everyone was free from the big isolation, and his uncle Ilir was out of the dark jail box, after spending his entire life there.

At the end, he was back home feeling free, and happy. They did not fall asleep at all that night, but celebrated with talking, singing, and dancing. After all they had so much to talk about. Since he left, things had taken a turn for the better in Albania. Dritan could feel the freedom, and it was good to be back. The summer was a great one for the whole family. Dritan's family accepted Mira happily in their arms without political grudges from the past, and Dritan was treated as one of the family boys at Mira's family. It might have been different if Communism did not collapse. Mira's father would not have accepted that relationship between them due to the fear of the system, the fear of losing his job and damaging his family. But the time had come where everyone was free to decide on their future without any fear on who to marry, and who to talk. Those days when Dritan's father's future was destroyed, due to his marriage to a "bourgeoisie family", were gone. Dr. Agim, who had graduated a few years after Dritan's parents at the same institute in Elbasan, did not know Dritan's parents from there, but he had heard about Agron in the early days of the Youth Communist movement. Anila's summer wedding turned into a grand reunion with cousins and relatives who had not spoken to their family for more than forty years of the Albanian Communist rule.

It was now time to move on and to forgive and forget. Dritan felt happy to see everyone. During his sister's wedding, Dritan and Mira announced their engagement. After Anila's wedding, Dritan started preparing his university application once again. He waited anxiously for a few months, and then he got the great news that he had been longing to hear. The young man had finally been admitted to the University of Fine Arts in Albania. With all the rejections and what he had gone through, this was a dream come true. Now that the Albanian dictatorship collapsed, there was no more unfair selection based on family backgrounds but on pure talent. Everyone who knew the young artist was happy for this wonderful news. At the university, Dritan, a mature student, was the eldest among his classmates. He enrolled with excitement and enthusiasm at the Tirana Fine Art Faculty. Finally, his dream had become a reality. To his surprise, a few of his art high-school friends had moved on with their lives and had become art professors in the faculty. Those academic years were the best in Dritan's life. Together with Mira, who also restarted her remaining Italian language studies, he enjoyed the open and independent thinking of his art subjects, and he did very well in all his courses.

# Chapter XIV

## A Hard Goodbye

During his school years, Dritan worked hard on various art projects. He often stayed till past-midnight on his art assignments and at times would try to keep himself awake through the night by drinking hot beverages. Soon after graduation, the talented artist started taking part in some art exhibitions around the country. In a few of those art shows, Dritan won different awards at the national level. It was a feeling of accomplishment and a new beginning. Although things were going well, the young man began planning for a more ambitious future for himself. Dritan and Mira's marriage followed after, and this was a happy time for everyone in his family, especially for his mother, Bardha. She had always been his mentor and a supporter of his dreams. However, now that him and Mira had seen a glimpse of the world, they had hopes of furthering their studies abroad. But telling his family and his mother that he had plans to leave again, was hard in Dritan's mind.

One evening when Dritan broke the news, his mother Bardha did not seem surprised. She dreamed that Dritan would further his art studies even if he had to go abroad to accomplish this. She was also proud with Mira's ambitions and achievements and would fully support their decision. They both were young, full of ambitions and ideas, and had a strong desire to move to Canada. Dritan was glad that that conversation went well and his mother was so supportive and understanding. He had dreamed of that country during the harsh times under Albanian Communism. After all, it was Canada where his dad Agron had wanted to go all along. But however hard they had tried to search for information on him, they had never been able to find or to hear anything from anywhere. Agron had left more than forty years ago. The family had finally concluded that he never made it across the border that snowy night, just like hundreds of other unfortunate ones who disappeared without a trace during those days. Dritan decided to pursue his father's dream of going to Canada; a place that had been in his mind throughout his childhood. Knowing some English language, as well as Italian, both of them decided to apply, with high hopes and desire, to become Canadian Citizens. After more than a year of taking intensive English language private classes, and reading about Canada, they felt ready.

Step by step, by filling forms and applications, Dritan and Mira successfully passed all the legal requirements. While they were waiting for the immigration news, Bardha, who had begun to complain about constant headaches, was diagnosed with a malignant brain tumor. The news was shocking and devastating for all. Things just happened so quickly, and the situation worsened in a few months. With the help of Mira's father, the medical staff tried their best to alleviate her pain and deterioration with their limited supplies and experience in such a disease. That early winter, Bardha left her last wishes and died peacefully surrounded by her kids, and many friends and family. Although it was a cold November day, Bardha's funeral was a big one. Over her entire life she had rightfully earned the respect of the community. Bardha sacrificed all her life and education for her family and never bent down to be manipulated by the Albanian Communist dictatorship tactics, that pressured the weak into becoming spies and tools for their system. She kept her head down and with a smile smartly navigated the political dangers to avoid any further troubles for her family. She labored the fields all day to put food at the table and looked after her children and her elder parents without forgetting to pay regular visits to her incarcerated brother.

After things settled, it left a big emptiness for Dritan, his sister Anila, and uncle Ilir. He had just begun enjoying his days in freedom and was reconnecting with his younger sister Bardha. Now he was the last survivor among his siblings. Despite the fact that things were not the same anymore, days, weeks, and months passed quietly, but they kept longing anxiously for any news from across the ocean. One summer day, Dritan and Mira finally got the great news they had waited for. Their immigration request to Canada had been accepted partly due to their improved language skills and partly due to Dritan's solid art background, his art exhibitions, and his experiences. The family felt immense joy and happiness. "My mom would have loved this news too," -thought Dritan. Since the computer and the internet were in its early stages, and it was still a luxury for a  new democracy like Albania, they decided to do their research about Canada by making full use of a few remaining books that their local town library possessed. These few books had survived after they had passed the foreign books censorship test, during the days of the strict dictatorship. Even though many of them were more than fifty or sixty  years old encyclopedias  and nature books, it still gave them some basic information about where they were heading to.

# Chapter XV

## *New Future, New Beginning*

Within a few months, Dritan and his wife Mira packed some of their belongings and said their goodbyes to their families. Mira's parents, and her brothers, Dritan's sister Anila, and his uncle Ilir, were very emotional at their leaving. It was not an easy moment for Dritan and his wife as they departed on their new life journey with only two suitcases. After more than a day of flying, and a stopover in Toronto, they finally landed in Vancouver. It was a busy city with a blend of British architecture, and North American high-rises. Their happiness and excitement were indescribable. In the days and weeks that followed, the couple made different local and international friends. Slowly, many kindhearted Canadian families and university colleagues, guided and assisted them in different ways. A few gave them advice for getting a small place to settle, and some others donated second-hand furniture.

On numerous occasions, helpful people showed them how they could get around the big city. Looking at the kind Canadians, Dritan and Mira, who were expecting a baby, were humbled. Indeed, they felt grateful and never forgot that welcoming generosity. The arrival of baby Alba was a joyous one and with it came the sleepless nights and the new family adjustments. Dritan's and Mira's family overseas were as happy as them. When the new academic year began, Dritan with patience and determination re-enrolled at the Academy of Arts in one of the local provincial universities. His Albanian Art University degree was not recognized in Canada, and he had to redo it again. What an undertaking for his age. Although Dritan was frustrated and disappointed in having to repeat his university from the very beginning, he managed to find the motivation to continue his passion and his dream. This education was another beginning in one of the Bachelor of Arts degree programs. Dritan felt honored, lucky and responsible. In the evenings and weekends, he worked for many years at a few part-time jobs such as pizza deliveries and sometimes waitressing at an Italian restaurant, in the shopping district of the downtown area. At the same time, he also found time to help Mira with baby Alba and with the chores at home, while Mira practiced cooking and trying new recipes with her international friends.

Mira had also enjoyed her parent's short visits from Albania. Having Agim and Diana over for a few months had been a great help especially with Alba. With many ups and downs and countless sleepless nights, Dritan balanced school, work, guests, and family responsibilities, and managed to do well in his studies. After all, some of these art classes were a repeat of ones he had done at the University of Arts in Albania. Mira had indeed been a big help in all of his achievements. With her degree in Italian translation, she was able to locate a job as a document translator for a Canadian-Italian Import-Export company that allowed her to work flexible hours and sometimes work from home. After a few years, Dritan completed his postgraduate program and became an art teacher at a local college. He felt that his persistence, endurance, and hard work, had finally paid off. While he enjoyed teaching art to the students, the ambitious man continued taking part in different art exhibitions and volunteering events around the world. These art shows were much different than the ones that he used to get rejected in participating during his childhood in the dictatorial Communist Albania. This trip for a major art exhibition in Los Angeles that he had just finished was another one of them. A loud bang shook Dritan suddenly and woke him from his daydreaming...

The plane from Los Angeles had landed safely at the Vancouver International Airport. The collective polite clapping from the passengers, made him feel at home. It was a simple gesture of the Canadian appreciation towards the captain of the plane for a safe landing. From a distance, he saw his wife Mira and his daughter Alba waiting impatiently for a hug. His little girl was holding her small favorite teddy bear "Googan." Dritan smiled. After he had passed through the usual immigration procedures, he was in their arms. It was a great feeling coming home to his new adopted country. Although things had gone well for Dritan, he had never forgotten his birthplace. In the last twenty years, Albania had been moving forward slowly but confidently in the path of freedom and democracy. Since his departure, Dritan and Mira kept in regular touch with their families and on occasion they helped them a bit financially with the little money he and Mira could save on occasions. Sometimes Dritan called his sister Anila and his uncle Ilir, who lived with Anila's family. His uncle, although greatly dismayed and disappointed about Albanian political bickering and corruption, was appreciating the little pleasures of freedom near the magnificent lake, while living with his only niece, Anila.

136

He was always excited to hear from Dritan and kept writing regularly to them in Canada with questions and interest in North America. Hearing the news that Dritan and Mira were inviting him for a visit to Canada, had brought greater happiness and curiosity. Indeed, the man had been a symbol of endurance. In his later years, Ilir received a settlement for his decades of hardship in jail, and a small pension from the new democratic government. Dritan thought about his grandparents, his father, and his mom. They did not live long enough to see their boys' humble achievements in his newly adopted country. However, they would be proud of him and surely felt good that he lives his life in freedom and did not suffer the same unfortunate fate as them. After his mom's death, his sister Anila had found a small keepsake with some old Communist currency and a note: "for my daughter Anila and Dritan's Art School...Bardha's dreams had been realized. He remembered his grandfather's Kreshnik advice and smiled. "Have deep faith in your dream Dritan, work hard with pleasure and passion, and wait for the right moment to seize. Don't get disheartened. Your day will come." Indeed, his day had finally come.

# ABOUT THE AUTHOR

Altin Dervishi was born and raised in the beautiful touristic city of Pogradec, Albania, South East Europe, during the forty years of the Albanian Communist isolation. For the last sixteen years, Altin has lived in Peterborough, Ontario, Canada with his family. "Art Passion...Denied!" is based on a few different true stories of the unjust Albanian dictatorship and the prosecutions of many good families including talented artists. This is Altin's second illustrative book for early teens interested in South-East European history. His first book "Flying To The Land Of Freedom," came in 2013.

140

Made in the USA
Lexington, KY
20 December 2019